Tapping Solutions: tapping scripts for stress management, weight loss, energy healing and more that you can use today! (inspired by Nick Ortner, Gary Craig, William Lee and Judith Orloff)

By Anthony Anholt

Copyright © 2013 by Anthony Anholt

Discover these other titles by Anthony Anholt:

The Isometric Exercise Bible

The Bodyweight Exercise Bible

The Abdominal Exercise Bible

Jump Rope Workouts

The Breathing Exercise Bible

Disclaimer

This book is for educational purposes only and is not intended to be a substitute for professional counseling, therapy or medical treatment. Nothing in this book is intended to diagnose or treat any pathology or diseased condition of the mind or body. The author and publisher will not be held responsible for any results of reading or applying this information. This book is presented as is and should not be taken for medical advice.

Table Of Contents

How Meridian Tapping Can Help You	5
Some Notes on Terminology	7
The Origins of Energy Healing	9
How Meridian Tapping Works	13
Meridian Tapping and the Subconscious Mind	15
The Importance of Deep Breathing	19
The Energy Healing Points of your Body	23
How to Perform EFT Tapping	27
Your First EFT Tapping Script	33
A Tapping Solution for ...	39
A Tapping Solution for Stress Management	41
A Tapping Solution for Weight Loss	49
A Tapping Solution for Headaches	57
A Tapping Solution for Sleep and Insomnia	61
A Tapping Solution for Happiness	67
A Tapping Solution for Creativity	75
A Tapping Solution for Shyness	83
A Tapping Solution for Procrastination	91
A Tapping Solution for Confidence	97
A Tapping Solution for Making Life Easier	103
A Tapping Solution for Love	111

Your Journey is Just Beginning	119
FAQ	121
Other Books of Interest	127
About The Author	129
One Last Thing	131

How Meridian Tapping Can Help You

Seek the outstanding mental conflict in the person, give him the remedy that will overcome that conflict and all the hope and encouragement you can, then the virtue within him will itself do all the rest. - Dr. Edward Bach

No matter who we are or what our current station is in life we all have a desire for self-improvement. Deep down we all know we have things we want to work on, personal mountains we want to climb. However despite our personal desire to improve ourselves, despite our knowledge that our lives would in some cases be vastly improved if we followed through, few of us do. The reality is that real change is hard. As a result an entire industry devoted to personal improvement has sprung up. Browse through the self-help section of any bookstore and you will likely find books on the following topics:

- How to manage stress
- Lose Weight NOW! (a very popular one)
- Get what you want in life
- Release yourself from fear and self-doubt
- How to make more money
- How to quit smoking/drinking
- Overcome anger and resentments
- Learn to be happy
- How to become a more dynamic individual
- Get in shape now!

- Learn to unleash your personal power
- Get that promotion now!
- How to overcome fear and depression

And on and on it goes. Obviously I can't be sure what aspect you would like to change and improve about yourself, but I'm willing to bet there's something. None of us are perfect. What's more I'm willing to bet you've put in some real time and effort in the past only to come up short. Why is making positive changes in our lives seemingly so hard? Is there anything we can do to make it easier?

This is where the technique of meridian tapping comes in. Often known by other names, including energy healing, EFT (emotional freedom technique) tapping or just plain tapping; meridian tapping allows you to literally re-program your brain in order to remove the hidden beliefs and emotional blockages that are likely holding you back. This technique is very easy to learn and can be self-administered (although you can see a therapist if you wish) almost anywhere you have a few minutes. People all over the world have taken advantage of this method and have vastly improved their lives in many disparate areas as a result. The only question you need to ask yourself is: are you ready to join them? Are you ready to break your own invisible bonds and become all you know you can be? If so read on, I've got something to show you ;).

Some Notes on Terminology

A rose by any other name would smell as sweet – from William Shakespeare's Romeo and Juliet

There are many different names and variations of tapping. Some of these include emotional freedom technique or EFT, meridian tapping and energy healing. I use these terms as well as others pretty much interchangeably even though other books may use them differently. For me these differences are immaterial as the essential technique is the same. Phrases are stated while various energy points of the body are tapped to achieve a desired result. Do not get hung up on the terminology. The melody may be different but the song is the same.

The Origins of Energy Healing

Health is not a condition of matter, but of mind.
- Mary Baker Eddy

All of us, whether we are aware of it or not, typically react in a physical way to deal with some kind of emotional trauma. When you are stressed how often do you find yourself massaging your temples? If you see something shocking doesn't your hand almost involuntarily leap to touch your mouth? Is not the most common way to soothe a baby to touch it and give it a gentle massage? What is going on here?

The truth is that our minds are much more than our physical brain. The mind encompasses and uses our entire body (and probably much more) in order to think and feel. With respect to emotion and trauma our mind literally stores them in our body. This is why we feel tension in our shoulders or butterflies in our stomach. These sensations are simply physical manifestations of what our mind is feeling and perceiving. This is why touching or massaging certain spots on our body can bring relief.

At some point in the past wise men and women from different cultures began to observe that massaging certain points of the body seemed to have more of an effect than others. This is what the Chinese started to do over 3700 years ago when they developed the idea that all living things possess a life force that flows along meridians in the body. Called "Chi" or "Qi" this life force is vital to a healthy mind and body. The root of all illness, in this view, is when these energy flows become blocked. Applying physical pressure (known as acupressure) or physically inserting needles (known as acupuncture) at certain meridian points can restore the energy flow and thereby make the body healthy again.

The Chinese are probably the most famous ancient culture to observe and make use of the body's natural energy flows, but they were not the only ones. For example a 5000-year-old mummy was discovered frozen in a glacier along the Italian border with Austria. What was interesting though was that this mummy appeared to have been treated with various tattoos along various known acupuncture points. The Ebers Papyrus from Egypt was written over 3500 years ago and yet it describes the energy channels that are not unlike Chinese meridians. One of the theories as to why the Indian elephant could be tamed whereas its African counterpart was not is that the ancient Indians were aware of acupressure points and were able to make use of them to calm and train the great beasts. There are many other examples but I think you get the idea. The concept that the body possesses flowing life energy and that this can be used to heal has been around for a long time.

In the west the first attempt to bring this ancient knowledge into the modern world was probably in a book entitled "Acupuncture: The Ancient Chinese Art of Healing" by Felix Mann in 1962. Mann had long been fascinated by the potential he saw in acupuncture and other natural healing techniques and this was the first attempt to document them for modern eyes. His book inspired a chiropractor named George Goodheart Jr. to explore the link between the mind and body and how it affects healing. Through his work Goodheart became acutely aware that it was often the patient's mental state that was the determining factor in how quickly they would respond to his treatments. As a chiropractor it was only natural for him to begin exploring the body's energy points and tapping. Although he made many insights into the field his most significant contribution was forming a study group and one of the students who joined it, Roger Callahan.

A pioneer in cognitive and behavior therapies Roger Callahan was a psychologist who was open to trying new therapies with his patients. As he had studied under Goodheart he was aware of the mind body connection and how it could be used to heal. However he didn't fully appreciate its power until he began treating a patient named Mary. Here's what happened.

For over a year and a half Callahan had been seeing Mary in order to provide treatment for her extreme phobia of water. Her fear was so great that she couldn't even get into a bathtub without it triggering an anxiety attack. Callahan tried every tool in his therapeutic toolkit to help her (including suggestion, placebo, clinical hypnosis, rational-emotive, behavioral therapy, distraction techniques, systematic desensitization and progressive relaxation) but nothing worked. Despite his best efforts Mary couldn't even approach a swimming pool that was near his office or even allow water to touch her body without a major episode being triggered.

During one session however Mary mentioned that she often got a sick feeling in the pit of her stomach whenever she thought of water. Through his work with Goodheart Callahan knew that there was an acupuncture point located directly below the eye that is thought to be linked to the stomach meridian. He had her tap on that point in the hopes that it would help her with her stomach queasiness. What happened next, however, was totally unexpected.

Mary did as she was asked and tapped under her eyes. However this action not only relieved her stomach symptoms, but it also removed her fear of water as well! The change was so sudden that Callahan assumed that Mary must have been playing some kind of joke. His skepticism turned to shock as Mary leapt up from her chair and ran towards a nearby swimming pool. Without any fear she entered the pool and walked until the water came up to her waist. She didn't go any deeper as she couldn't swim, so she just stood there laughing as she splashed water on her face. In this case the results from just a few minutes of tapping were staggering. What had just occurred and why? Let's look at that now.

How Meridian Tapping Works

Treat the cause not the effect.
- Dr. Edward Bach

In some ways your brain is almost like a computer. The main task of this computer is to make cause and effect associations in order to better understand the world around you. When you are a baby these associations are usually very straightforward. For example touching a hot stove leads to intense pain, which is undesirable. Your brain then wires or programs itself to associate a hot stove (cause) with potential pain (the effect). It will also likely create other cause and effect associations in order to avoid pain in the future. For example hot stove (cause) evokes fear or wariness (effect) in order to avoid the pain.

As we get older these cause and effect associations and responses become much more sophisticated but the underlying principle is the same. Where we get into problems though as adults is that the cause and effect responses that our brains create may be far from optimal. For example your brain may program itself to associate stress at work (cause) with drinking (effect). Meaning you develop a pre-programmed response to deal with stress with drinking. I think it goes without saying that drinking is not the optimal method by which to handle stress and this association is far from ideal. Over-eating, self-doubt, smoking, constantly getting into poor relationships, these are all examples of the problems we can create for ourselves when our brain is programmed with poor cause and effect associations.

What is even more interesting though is that our brain can often use a pre-existing cause and effect association in completely unrelated situations. This appears to be what happened to Mary. Although it's possible that she had some kind of trauma in her childhood related to water I tend to doubt it. I'm sure that a psychologist as sharp as Callahan could have helped her through issues surrounding a near drowning episode, for example. More likely Mary experienced some kind of trauma in her youth that created a powerful cause and effect association in her brain. At some point Mary's brain began to invoke this association every time she was near or thought of water. It is almost as if her brain had a faulty program. This is why the mere thought of water would throw her into a panic.

If this is the case how did tapping help Mary re-program her mind? The answer is that the action of tapping made use of the mind body connection. Our brains are in our heads, but our minds encompass our entire body (and some would say much more). In this case the act of physically tapping on this key healing point permanently scrambled the faulty cause and effect association that Mary had developed in her brain. This is one of the big keys to understanding the power of tapping. It gives you the power to erase old cause and effect associations and replace them with new ones.

Meridian Tapping and the Subconscious Mind

It's repetition of affirmations that leads to belief and once that belief becomes a deep conviction, things begin to happen. - Muhammad Ali

In order to more fully understand why tapping is so powerful it is important to understand how your mind works in order to achieve desirable goals. This is a point that a lot of other books on tapping seem to miss yet; it is a vital point to understand. Let me explain it by way of a somewhat nerdy analogy.

In some ways your mind is not unlike the good ship Enterprise of Star Trek fame. It has a captain in the form of the volatile James T. Kirk as well as an engineer (Scotty) toiling away in the bowels of the ship. Although it is the captain that gives the orders it is actually Scotty who carries them out. The key point here though is that Scotty is essentially blind. When given an order he will always attempt to carry out the order, whether it is actually true or not. So, if Kirk declares "Klingons in sight! Raise shields!" with his usual Shatner-esque passion Scotty will do just that, whether the Klingons exist or not.

The problem for Scotty though is that Kirk is somewhat volatile and often gives orders that are contradictory or said without any real conviction. What does Scotty do when he receives the contradictory orders "Warp 7 Mr. Scott" immediately followed by "Full reverse!"?

Most likely he does just what you would do. He ignores the contradictory orders and simply goes on following whatever previous instructions he had programmed into his computer. In the same vein if he gets a half-hearted order such as "Activate shields, I guess" delivered with no sense of urgency Scotty, who is busy with a thousand other tasks, is likely to ignore this as well.

Your mind essentially works the same way, with Kirk and Scotty standing in for your conscious and subconscious mind. Your conscious mind is what you are aware of what right now as you read this. Thoughts and feelings constantly flow through it and it is nominally in charge. On the other hand, most people are utterly unaware of their subconscious mind, although this is where things really get done. Let's say your conscious mind decides that you want to loose 10 pounds. This message is relayed to your subconscious mind. Are you serious though? If your conscious mind later relays eat that big piece of cake, 5 minutes later your subconscious mind will literally throw up its hands. What's worse though, is that if you do this enough your subconscious mind will learn to ignore this order. In fact, it will likely create a cause and effect relationship that says, "When I say I want to lose weight I don't really mean it, so just eat another piece of cake". When you get this thought programmed into your subconscious it can be very hard to change. Have you wondered why will power isn't enough to lose weight? This is why. If your conscious mind says it wants something but your subconscious is not on board based on past experience it is very hard to change your behavior.

Let's take another look at the Mary example through the lenses of this conscious/subconscious mind paradigm. For whatever reason, Mary's subconscious mind associated the mere idea of water with extreme distress. As soon as her conscious mind became aware of water her subconscious mind would immediately follow this false program and go into full panic mode. As long as that false cause and effect association was active in her subconscious mind it wouldn't matter what her conscious mind would say to it. This same process applies to losing weight and any other subject you can think of. If your subconscious mind has a different program it will not accept it either. It doesn't matter what your conscious mind says.

What the physical act of tapping does is scrambles the pre-existing programming that often exists in your subconscious mind. It allows Scotty to purge his goal-setting computer and allow new instructions to be accepted. It allowed Mary to break the terrifying associations she had made with water. It can allow you to break your programming related to smoking, weight loss, or any other issue. This is why tapping can be so powerful.

The Importance of Deep Breathing

Improper breathing is a common cause of ill health. Changing your breathing patterns can affect and improve you mentally, emotionally and physically – Andrew Weil, M.D.

Before we put it all together and explain exactly how to tap to improve your life I feel it is important to cover a topic that most tapping books gloss over if they even mention it at all. This topic is the absolute importance of engaging in proper, deep breathing as you tap. Deep, slow, controlled breathing is critical to creating a pliable mind that is open to change. A calm mind is much more receptive to suggestions than one that is stressed. Here's why.

Yoga masters have long believed that breathing is what connects the mind with the body. For most people how they are breathing is a direct reflection of how they feel. For example when your mind is calm and relaxed so is your breath. However when you are experiencing fear and stress your breathing typically speeds up and becomes much shallower. In fact many yogi masters can get so good at reading a person's breath it almost appears as if they are reading their mind. The lesson here though is that unconsciously your mind controls your breath.

What most people don't realize though is that the mind/breath connection is a two way street. By taking conscious control of your breathing you have the ability to calm your mind. For example let's say you are feeling a great deal of fear and stress because you have a public speaking engagement. By controlling your breath by taking deeper, slower breaths through your nose you can actually calm your mind and significantly lower if not eliminate that fear.

How exactly do you control your breath? Whenever you feel the need to calm your mind (or when engaging in a round of tapping) focus on these factors:

- Always breathe through your nose. Your nose is designed to be the primary method by which we inhale and exhale air. Breathing through your mouth is meant only as a backup, such as when you are sick or need to take in great quantities of oxygen in a stressful situation. It is this last point that is key. Back in caveman days breathing through your mouth was most often associated with hunting. You were either running very fast to get or to avoid becoming food. This legacy is still with us today (talk about a powerful cause and effect association!) and why mouth breathing triggers a "fight or flight" response in your mind. This is why it is critically important to breathe through your nose at all times, but particularly in stressful situations.
- Breathe using your diaphragm. Your diaphragm is the large muscle that separates your thoracic cavity (which contains your lungs, heart, and ribs) from your abdominal cavity. When your

diaphragm is relaxed it extends upwards into your lungs, which collapses them. Engaging your diaphragm muscles flattens them out which enlarges your lungs and causes air to enter. The reason you want this to happen is that your lungs are largest at their base; therefore breathing this way (deep, diaphragmatic breathing) allows more oxygen to enter. Shallow breathing, meaning breathing from the top of your lungs, also triggers the fight or flight response. Only deep diaphragmatic breathing calms the mind.

There is so much more I could say about the value of deep breathing that I actually wrote a book about it. However the above gives you the basics. In order to get the most out of meridian tapping do not neglect your breath. A calm mind is a pliable mine, which is exactly what you want in order to get the most out of your tapping experience.

22

The Energy Healing Points of your Body

Every patient carries his or her own doctor inside.
- Albert Schweitzer

According to modern practitioners of acupuncture and acupressure there are hundreds of potential energy healing points and meridian lines in the human body. As this is an introductory guide we will be focusing on what is considered to be the 9 major energy points. Please keep in mind that these are only a starting point. As I have said repeatedly throughout this book you are a unique individual and it is entirely possible that as you "make tapping your own" you will find energy points that work for you. How do you find these points? Simply by listening to your body. If you find that you feel greater relief by tapping in the middle of your forehead then feel free to do so. Your ultimate goal should be to make tapping solutions that work for you. Regardless of where you wind up in your tapping journey you need to start somewhere, which is what the guide below is intended to do.

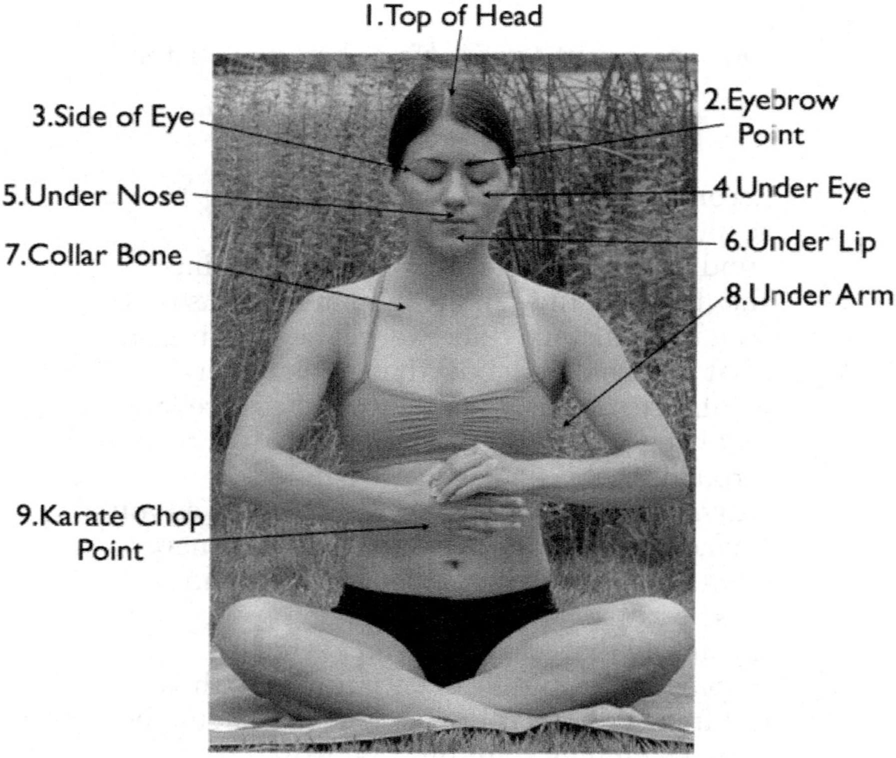
1.Top of Head
3.Side of Eye
2.Eyebrow Point
5.Under Nose
4.Under Eye
7.Collar Bone
6.Under Lip
8.Under Arm
9.Karate Chop Point

1. Top of Head – This tapping point is commonly considered to be the meeting point for all meridians in the body. This is why it can be such a powerful healing point for any issue you may be facing.
2. Eyebrow Point – This point is often associated with your bladder and it can lead to anxiety, futility, frustration and trauma when it is out of balance. Tapping here should help to engender feelings of hope, harmony and peace.
3. Side of Eye – This healing point is associated with the gall bladder and it

can lead to a feeling of being overly judgmental as well as resentment when it is in a low frequency state. Tapping on this point should help you experience a sense of kindness, tolerance, love and just a general sense of well-being.
4. Under Eye – This point is associated with the stomach and it can be responsible for such feelings as fear, anxiety, emptiness, greed and worry. Tapping to correct this should lead to a feeling of contentment, tranquility and trust in the world at large.
5. Under Nose – This healing point is generally not considered to be associated with any particular organ but it can lead to feelings of cowardice and insecurity when in a low frequency state. Tapping this point can restore a sense of strength, pride and courage.
6. Under Lip – Feelings of vulnerability, embarrassment and shame are the negative aspects associated with this point. Tapping here can restore a sense of security and centered pride.
7. Collar Bone – This point is associated with the kidney. Feelings of loneliness, shame and anxiety may result when an energy blockage occurs at this point. Restoration of the energy flow here should result in feelings of self-acceptance and calm.
8. Under Arm – Associated with the spleen, energy blockages here can result in an inability to easily absorb new information as well as anxiety and low self-esteem. Restoring the energy

balance here can help lead to an open mind as well as feelings of confidence and security.
9. Karate Chop Point – This healing point is associated with the small intestine and it can provoke thoughts of feeling divided and confused as well as sadness and vulnerability when it is out of balance. Restoring balance here should manifest feelings of decisiveness, clarity and joy in the practitioner.

How to Perform EFT Tapping

Health is not a condition of matter, but of Mind.
- Mary Baker Eddy

Now that you understand the importance of proper deep breathing, the power of your subconscious mind as well as your body's energy meridians we can now put it all together and actually do it. Every meridian tapping script you will do follows the same pattern and is made up of three steps. Let's analyze each in detail now.

Step One: Self-Assessment

That which is measured improves. That which is measured and reported improves exponentially - Karl Pearson

This is a step that many tapping books I've read seem to miss; yet I feel it is vitally important. Before you perform a round of tapping you should take a moment and simply mediate on the issue you are dealing with. How do you feel about it? Does it still have a strong hold on you, or do you feel you are making progress? Give yourself a ranking on a scale of 1 to 10. Write this number down in a journal and be honest with yourself. Always remember that it is impossible to deceive yourself. Remember your sub-conscious mind, if it gets an order that is not delivered with any kind of conviction it is likely to ignore it. This defeats the whole purpose of the exercise.

One point I want to stress is that you should NEVER feel bad if your self-assessment number doesn't change. Experiencing change through tapping is not a goal or a race to be won. You may stay with lower frequency statements for some time if the false cause and effect associations your brain has made in the past are particularly strong. Just remember that so long as you are making statements that feel true you WILL make progress, no matter what frequency you are at.

Step Two: Set-Up Statement

This is where you declare to yourself and your subconscious mind the issue that you intend to work on. As you make your declaration you will tap lightly with two or three fingers on the karate chop point. The set-up statement should always correlate with your self-assessment number whether it is high frequency or low frequency. What I mean by this will become clear when you read the sample tapping scripts that follow.

One thing that many people find striking about low frequency set-up statements (this holds true for reminder phrases as well) is that they can appear to be quite negative. People often recoil from this as the modern self-help industry has flooded the market with countless books, articles and video's condemning negative thoughts in any form. Why make use of them at all?

It all comes back to your subconscious mind and truly believing what you are saying. If you are feeling negative or down it is important to express that. That is your starting point and there is nothing wrong with it. If you try and implant a false belief that your sub-conscious finds completely phony it will simply reject it immediately. It is simply impossible to lie to yourself.

Another point is that so-called "negative" thoughts are not necessarily a bad thing. This is why I tend to call them "low frequency" as opposed to "negative". Being honest about low frequency thoughts and feelings are important for two reasons:

- Low frequency thoughts helps us to build contrasts and sharpen our focus onto what we really do want
- They are vital in allowing ourselves to acknowledge our true feelings at any one moment.

Can you truly experience a sunny day without knowing what night is? Stop seeing low frequency thoughts as being negative or undesirable. They are neither good nor bad. They simply are.

Step Three: Reminder Phrase

This is the phrase you will say to your subconscious mind as you tap three to seven times on the various energy-healing points around your body. Again this phrase will change depending on your self-evaluation.

Additional Notes

Once you have finished a round of tapping it is time to go back to step one and re-evaluate yourself. If you feel your thoughts and feelings have moved into a higher frequency change your self-assessment number, set-up statement and reminder phrase to reflect this. If you feel the same simply repeat the process. I suggest you complete three rounds of tapping at a minimum, although you can do more if you have the time. Below are some additional notes you should keep in mind:

- You should tap with the same pressure you would apply if you were to make a drumming sound on a table with your fingertips. You should feel it, but it shouldn't cause you any discomfort.
- Sometimes you might experience what is called a "One minute wonder" in which whatever affliction you are tapping for (much like what occurred with Mary and water) magically disappears.

- As you tap you may find sensations or feelings on other parts of your body as well. If so acknowledge them and recognize that your body and subconscious mind are likely trying to tell you something. I would suggest that you add these points to your tapping cycle and see if it doesn't help you.
- You should never be afraid of doing your EFT tapping incorrectly. There is no such thing. The only way you can do it wrong is by not doing it.

What follows are some suggested EFT tapping solutions for common ailments and conditions. Always remember though that these meridian tapping scripts are suggestions only and that once you get the hang of it you can modify them as you please, or even make up completely new ones following the self-evaluation/setup statement/reminder phrase model. The more you make whatever tapping solution you are using your own the faster your healing will likely be.

Your First EFT Tapping Script

The doctor of the future will give no medicine but will interest his patients in the care of the human frame, in diet and in the cause and prevention of disease.
- Thomas Edison

At this point you are ready to try your first EFT tapping script. From my experience there is a good chance you are feeling skeptical about this whole process and whether meridian tapping can work for you. If this is the case this is the first EFT script you will do. If, on the other hand, you are feeling extremely excited about this technique and want to get to it I suggest you skip this step and move onto a script which is more relevant for you.

Step One – Self-Evaluation

In a notebook write down, on a scale of 1 to 10 how skeptical you are about the ability of meridian tapping to help you (with 10 being extremely skeptical and 1 being excited about the possibilities). Don't think about it too hard. The first number that pops into your head is likely the correct one.

A Tapping Script for Tapping Skepticism Levels 8 - 10

Begin by using the fingers of one of your hands to tap the karate chop point of the other while you say three times:

"Even though I don't believe this will work for me, I deeply and completely love and accept myself"

Now use two fingers and gently tap each of the following healing points below three to seven times by saying the following reminder phrase:

"It won't work for me"

A complete round of tapping for this reminder phrase would look like this:

Top of Head – "It won't work for me"
Eyebrow Point - "It won't work for me"
Side of Eye - "It won't work for me"
Under Eye - "It won't work for me"
Under Nose - "It won't work for me"
Under Lip - "It won't work for me"
Collar Bone - "It won't work for me"
Under Arm - "It won't work for me"
Top of Head - "It won't work for me"

Once you have completed this round of tapping re-evaluate yourself again and do another round of tapping appropriate to your level of skepticism unless you have already completed three rounds of tapping.

A Tapping Script for Tapping Skepticism
Levels 5 - 7

If you feel your mind opening up to the possibilities that tapping offers but are not yet completely sold on the idea it is time to use set-up and reminder phrases that are more neutral.

Begin by using the fingers of one of your hands to tap the karate chop point of the other while you say three times:

"I believe this could work for me and I deeply and completely love and accept myself"

Now use two fingers and gently tap each of the following healing points below three to seven times by saying the following reminder phrase:

"I believe meridian tapping might work for me"

A complete round of tapping for this reminder phrase would look like this:

Top of Head – "I believe meridian tapping might work for me"
Eyebrow Point - "I believe meridian tapping might work for me"
Side of Eye - "I believe meridian tapping might work for me"
Under Eye - "I believe meridian tapping might work for me"
Under Nose - "I believe meridian tapping might work for me"
Under Lip - "I believe meridian tapping might work for me"

Collar Bone - "I believe meridian tapping might work for me"
Under Arm - "I believe meridian tapping might work for me"
Top of Head - "I believe meridian tapping might work for me"

Once you have completed this round of tapping re-evaluate yourself again and do another round of tapping appropriate to your level of skepticism unless you have already completed three rounds of tapping.

A Tapping Script for Tapping Skepticism Levels 1 - 4

If you are feeling excited about the power of tapping and what it can do for you move onto this set-up statement:

"Meridian tapping is working for me, I am feeling better and stronger and I completely love and accept myself"

Now use two fingers and gently tap each of the following healing points below three to seven times by saying the following reminder phrase:

"Meridian tapping is working for me and I feel fantastic"

A complete round of tapping for this reminder phrase would look like this:

Top of Head – "Meridian tapping is working for me and I feel fantastic"
Eyebrow Point - "Meridian tapping is working for me and I feel fantastic"
Side of Eye - "Meridian tapping is working for me and I feel fantastic"
Under Eye - "Meridian tapping is working for me and I feel fantastic"
Under Nose - "Meridian tapping is working for me and I feel fantastic"
Under Lip - ""Meridian tapping is working for me and I feel fantastic"
Collar Bone - "Meridian tapping is working for me and I feel fantastic"
Under Arm - "Meridian tapping is working for me and I feel fantastic"

Top of Head - "Meridian tapping is working for me and I feel fantastic"

Once you have completed this round of tapping re-evaluate yourself again and do another round of tapping appropriate to your level of skepticism unless you have already completed three rounds of tapping.

Once you have completed three rounds of tapping you can stop, although you can do more if you feel like it and have the time. One point that I want to stress as it is so important is that you should never judge yourself or feel bad if you complete three rounds of tapping and your self-evaluation is stuck in a low frequency state. There is nothing wrong with this. Always remember that "negative" is not bad, it simply is. If you are not feeling it that particular day simply accept how you are feeling without judgment and move on. Know that you are likely making progress simply by putting in the effort of tapping and acknowledging your feelings. This point is so important I feel the need to emphasize it again:

Do NOT let it bother you in the least if you remain in a state of low frequency after completing three rounds of energy tapping. This is simply a reflection of how you are feeling that day and you are to be commended for being honest with yourself.

A Tapping Solution for ...

Health is a large word. It embraces not the body only, but the mind and spirit as well...and not today's pain or pleasure alone, but the whole being and outlook of a man. - James H. West

What follows are some specific energy healing tapping scripts for specific conditions. All of them follow the model set out by the sample script listed above, meaning they all involve self-evaluation followed by a round of tapping based on that evaluation. Even if you are not interested in an "EFT (emotional freedom technique) for weight loss" tapping script I believe you will gain tremendous value by reading ALL of these sample scripts. The reason being that once you are comfortable with how these scripts are set up it should be that much easier for you to create your own. As always your goal is to mold your tapping scripts to your own unique character so that they work for you. If you are always willing to listen to your body and experiment I am confident that you will find a meridian tapping script that will work for you.

A Tapping Solution Script for Stress Management

The greatest weapon against stress is our ability to choose one thought over another – William James

One of the biggest mental issues that we all face in the modern world is an overwhelming feeling of stress. Stress is not a bad thing in and of itself so long as you use it as an impetus to get stronger and improve your life. As others have noted, without intense pressure and stress a lump of coal would never turn into a diamond. Stress only becomes an issue when it is overwhelming and prevents you from taking positive action. This is what this energy healing script is meant to do, move you from a position of inaction to empowered action.

Self-Evaluation

The first thing to do is to think about something specific that is bothering you and causing stress in your life. Think about how it makes you feel, both emotionally and physically. Now take out your notebook and write down on a scale of 1 to 10 how stressed you feel (10 being the maximum stress level and 1 the calmest). Depending on where you rank yourself begin a round of tapping as listed below.

Tapping Script for Stress Levels of 8 – 10

Begin by using the fingers of one of your hands to tap the karate chop point of the other while saying the following set up statement three times:

"Even though I am feeling extremely stressed out about my issue (you can insert your specific stress related issue here, if you wish), I deeply and completely love and accept myself"

Now use two fingers to tap each of the healing points below three to seven times saying the following reminder phrase:

"I'm all stressed out and this stress is real"

A complete round of tapping for this reminder phrase would look like this:

Top of Head – "I'm all stressed out and this stress is real"
Eyebrow Point - "I'm all stressed out and this stress is real"
Side of Eye - "I'm all stressed out and this stress is real"
Under Eye - "I'm all stressed out and this stress is real"
Under Nose - "I'm all stressed out and this stress is real"
Under Lip - "I'm all stressed out and this stress is real"
Collar Bone - "I'm all stressed out and this stress is real"
Under Arm - "I'm all stressed out and this stress is real"

Top of Head - "I'm all stressed out and this stress is real"

Once you have completed this round of tapping re-evaluate yourself again and do another round of tapping appropriate to your stress level unless you have already completed three rounds of tapping.

Tapping Script for a Stress Levels of 5 – 7

A stress level of 5 – 7 indicates that although the stress you are feeling is very real it is not paralyzing or overwhelming. Begin by using the fingers of one of your hands to tap the karate chop point of the other while saying the following set up statement three times:

"Even though I am feeling stressed out about my issue I am open to finding solutions and I can handle it"

Now use two fingers to tap each of the healing points below three to seven times saying the following reminder phrase:

"Although I am feeling stressed I know I can handle it"

A complete round of tapping for this reminder phrase would look like this:

Top of Head – "Although I am feeling stressed I know I can handle it"
Eyebrow Point - "Although I am feeling stressed I know I can handle it"
Side of Eye - "Although I am feeling stressed I know I can handle it"
Under Eye - "Although I am feeling stressed I know I can handle it"
Under Nose - "Although I am feeling stressed I know I can handle it"
Under Lip - "Although I am feeling stressed I know I can handle it"
Collar Bone - "Although I am feeling stressed I know I can handle it"

Under Arm - "Although I am feeling stressed I know I can handle it"
Top of Head - "Although I am feeling stressed I know I can handle it"

Once you have completed this round of tapping re-evaluate yourself again and do another round of tapping appropriate to your stress level unless you have already completed three rounds of tapping.

Tapping Script for a Stress Levels of 1 – 4

A stress level of 1 – 4 indicates that although you are feeling stress it is something you know you can handle and you are ready to take action to eliminate it all together. Begin by using the fingers of one of your hands to tap the karate chop point of the other while saying the following set up statement three times:

"Although I am experiencing stress I am strong and worthy and I know I am going to find a solution for my issue (insert your own particular issue here)"

Now use two fingers to tap each of the healing points below three to seven times saying the following reminder phrase:

"Although I am experiencing stress I know I will find a solution"

A complete round of tapping for this reminder phrase would look like this:

Top of Head – "Although I am experiencing stress I know I will find a solution"
Eyebrow Point - "Although I am experiencing stress I know I will find a solution"
Side of Eye - "Although I am experiencing stress I know I will find a solution"
Under Eye - "Although I am experiencing stress I know I will find a solution"
Under Nose - "Although I am experiencing stress I know I will find a solution"
Under Lip - "Although I am experiencing stress I know I will find a solution"

Collar Bone - "Although I am experiencing stress I know I will find a solution"
Under Arm - "Although I am experiencing stress I know I will find a solution"
Top of Head - "Although I am experiencing stress I know I will find a solution"

Once you have completed this round of tapping re-evaluate yourself again and do another round of tapping appropriate to your stress level unless you have already completed three rounds of tapping.

A Tapping Solution Script for Weight Loss

Your body can do anything – it's your brain you have to convince - unknown

Just by judging by the enormous size of the diet and weight loss industry there are very few of us who don't want to lose weight. If this is the case then why is it so hard? A big part of the problem is how we see ourselves through our self-image. Our conscious mind may decide to start eating better and exercising, but as you now know it doesn't matter if you subconscious mind doesn't see it that way, and for most of us, that's the problem. Our subconscious minds don't believe that you are serious about exercise, or that you really want to cut back on sweets. Changing your subconscious mind about this is what this weight loss script is all about.

Self-Evaluation

Think about your attempts to lose weight in the past and the reasons why you failed. Think about how this made you feel. Now write down in your notebook how confident you are on a scale of 1 to 10 that this time will be different. 1 being that you have no confidence that you will lose weight this time and 10 representing that every cell in your body believes that you can do it. Now let's get tapping.

Tapping Script for Weight Loss Levels of 1 - 4

Begin by using the fingers of one of your hands to tap the karate chop point of the other while saying the following set up statement three times:

"Even though I have had unhealthy food cravings in the past I deeply and completely love and accept myself"

Note that if you have particularly specific food cravings (such as chocolate bars or alcohol, for example) you can add them into this set up statement.

Now use two fingers to tap each of the healing points below three to seven times saying the following reminder phrase:

"I have deep cravings for unhealthy food and this feeling is real"

A complete round of tapping for this reminder phrase would look like this:

Top of Head – "I have deep cravings for unhealthy food and this feeling is real"
Eyebrow Point - "I have deep cravings for unhealthy food and this feeling is real"
Side of Eye - "I have deep cravings for unhealthy food and this feeling is real"
Under Eye - "I have deep cravings for unhealthy food and this feeling is real"
Under Nose - "I have deep cravings for unhealthy food and this feeling is real"

Under Lip - "I have deep cravings for unhealthy food and this feeling is real"
Collar Bone - "I have deep cravings for unhealthy food and this feeling is real"
Under Arm - "I have deep cravings for unhealthy food and this feeling is real"
Top of Head - "I have deep cravings for unhealthy food and this feeling is real"

Once you have completed this round of tapping re-evaluate yourself again and do another round of tapping appropriate to your stress level unless you have already completed three rounds of tapping.

Tapping Script for Weight Loss Levels of 5 - 7

Begin by using the fingers of one of your hands to tap the karate chop point of the other while saying the following set up statement three times:

"Even though I have had unhealthy food cravings in the past I believe I have the power to change them this time"

Now use two fingers to tap each of the healing points below three to seven times saying the following reminder phrase:

"My food cravings do not control me"

A complete round of tapping for this reminder phrase would look like this:

Top of Head – "My food cravings do not control me"
Eyebrow Point - "My food cravings do not control me"
Side of Eye - "My food cravings do not control me"
Under Eye - "My food cravings do not control me"
Under Nose - "My food cravings do not control me"
Under Lip - "My food cravings do not control me"
Collar Bone - "My food cravings do not control me"
Under Arm - "My food cravings do not control me"

Top of Head - "My food cravings do not control me"

Once you have completed this round of tapping re-evaluate yourself again and do another round of tapping appropriate to your stress level unless you have already completed three rounds of tapping.

Tapping Script for Weight Loss Levels of 8 - 10

Begin by using the fingers of one of your hands to tap the karate chop point of the other while saying the following set up statement three times:

"I do not crave fattening foods and I will take the necessary steps to lose weight"

Now use two fingers to tap each of the healing points below three to seven times saying the following reminder phrase:

"I will do what is required to lose weight and keep it off"

A complete round of tapping for this reminder phrase would look like this:

Top of Head – "I will do what is required to lose weight and keep it off"
Eyebrow Point - "I will do what is required to lose weight and keep it off"
Side of Eye -"I will do what is required to lose weight and keep it off"
Under Eye - "I will do what is required to lose weight and keep it off"
Under Nose - "I will do what is required to lose weight and keep it off"
Under Lip - "I will do what is required to lose weight and keep it off"
Collar Bone - "I will do what is required to lose weight and keep it off"
Under Arm - "I will do what is required to lose weight and keep it off"

Top of Head - "I will do what is required to lose weight and keep it off"

Once you have completed this round of tapping re-evaluate yourself again and do another round of tapping appropriate to your stress level unless you have already completed three rounds of tapping.

A Tapping Solution for Headaches

*A great wind is blowing, and that gives you either
imagination or a headache - Catherine the Great*

We all suffer from headaches from time to time. Meridian tapping has been known to cure headaches in some people almost instantly. I can't promise you those kinds of results, but I know that it is possible. As well these scripts can be easily modified to deal with other manifestations of pain, such as knee pain or even migraines. There really is no limit to what can be accomplished with energy healing.

Self-Evaluation

Concentrate on your headache and how severe it is. I would place an intense headache at the 8 to 10 end of the scale, whereas a 1 would represent a headache free state. Let's get started.

A Tapping Script for Headaches Levels of 8 - 10

Begin by using the fingers of one of your hands to tap the karate chop point of the other while saying the following set up statement three times:

"Even though I have this headache I deeply and completely accept myself"

Note that you can substitute headaches for any physical pain you might be experiencing.

Now use two fingers to tap each of the healing points below three to seven times saying the following reminder phrase:

"This headache is real"

A complete round of tapping for this reminder phrase would look like this:

Top of Head – "This headache is real"
Eyebrow Point – "This headache is real"
Side of Eye - "This headache is real"
Under Eye – "This headache is real"
Under Nose - "This headache is real"
Under Lip - "This headache is real"
Collar Bone - "This headache is real"
Under Arm - "This headache is real"
Top of Head - "This headache is real"

Once you have completed this round of tapping re-evaluate yourself again and do another round of tapping appropriate to your stress level unless you have already completed three rounds of tapping.

A Tapping Script for Headaches Levels of 5 - 7

Begin by using the fingers of one of your hands to tap the karate chop point of the other while saying the following set up statement three times:

"Even though I have this headache I believe I have the power to cure it"

Now use two fingers to tap each of the healing points below three to seven times saying the following reminder phrase:

"I have the power to cure it"

A complete round of tapping for this reminder phrase would look like this:

Top of Head – "I have the power to cure it"
Eyebrow Point – "I have the power to cure it"
Side of Eye - "I have the power to cure it"
Under Eye – "I have the power to cure it"
Under Nose - "I have the power to cure it"
Under Lip - "I have the power to cure it"
Collar Bone - "I have the power to cure it"
Under Arm - "I have the power to cure it"
Top of Head - "I have the power to cure it"

Once you have completed this round of tapping re-evaluate yourself again and do another round of tapping appropriate to your stress level unless you have already completed three rounds of tapping.

A Tapping Script for Headaches Levels of 1 - 4

Begin by using the fingers of one of your hands to tap the karate chop point of the other while saying the following set up statement three times:

"Even though I have this headache I am using my healing energy to cure it"

Now use two fingers to tap each of the healing points below three to seven times saying the following reminder phrase:

"My headache will soon be gone"

A complete round of tapping for this reminder phrase would look like this:

Top of Head – "My headache will soon be gone"
Eyebrow Point – "My headache will soon be gone"
Side of Eye - "My headache will soon be gone"
Under Eye – "My headache will soon be gone"
Under Nose - "My headache will soon be gone"
Under Lip - "My headache will soon be gone"
Collar Bone - "My headache will soon be gone"
Under Arm - "My headache will soon be gone"
Top of Head - "My headache will soon be gone"

Once you have completed this round of tapping re-evaluate yourself again and do another round of tapping appropriate to your stress level unless you have already completed three rounds of tapping.

A Tapping Solution for Sleep and Insomnia

The best cure for insomnia is to get a lot of sleep – W.C. Fields

The inability to fall asleep when we want to, otherwise known as insomnia, is an unfortunate condition we have all experienced at some point. The most common cause is simply an overactive mind that is worrying about anything and everything. As time passes and the clock keeps ticking our minds then focus on our inability to go to sleep, which makes matters even worse. These tapping scripts are designed to help your mind break free of these destructive patterns so that you can enjoy a good nights sleep.

Two other non-tapping suggestions I have for you is to try listening to some soft music or a boring podcast. The goal here is to focus your mind on something else besides your insomnia. Having a cold shower right before bed can be effective as well. The reason for this is that our bodies naturally cool down as part of the sleep cycle. A cold shower can help kick start this process. I suggest trying both of these techniques after you finish your tapping routine.

Self-Evaluation

How awake are you? Being wide-awake would give you a ranking of 10 whereas a 1 represents the stage where you are just about to drift off to dreamland. Write down where you are and start tapping at the appropriate level.

A Tapping Script for Sleep and Insomnia
Levels of 8 - 10

Begin by using the fingers of one of your hands to tap the karate chop point of the other while saying the following set up statement three times:

"Even though I have difficulty falling asleep I deeply and completely accept myself"

Now use two fingers to tap each of the healing points below three to seven times saying the following reminder phrase:

"It is hard to fall asleep"

A complete round of tapping for this reminder phrase would look like this:

Top of Head – "It is hard to fall asleep"
Eyebrow Point – "It is hard to fall asleep"
Side of Eye - "It is hard to fall asleep"
Under Eye – "It is hard to fall asleep"
Under Nose - "It is hard to fall asleep"
Under Lip - "It is hard to fall asleep"
Collar Bone - "It is hard to fall asleep"
Under Arm - "It is hard to fall asleep"
Top of Head - "It is hard to fall asleep"

Once you have completed this round of tapping re-evaluate yourself again and do another round of tapping appropriate to your stress level unless you have already completed three rounds of tapping.

A Tapping Script for Sleep and Insomnia Levels of 5 - 7

Begin by using the fingers of one of your hands to tap the karate chop point of the other while saying the following set up statement three times:

"Even though I am having difficulty sleeping my mind is calming itself and relaxing"

Now use two fingers to tap each of the healing points below three to seven times saying the following reminder phrase:

"I am beginning to feel sleepy"

A complete round of tapping for this reminder phrase would look like this:

Top of Head – "I am beginning to feel sleepy"
Eyebrow Point – "I am beginning to feel sleepy"
Side of Eye - "I am beginning to feel sleepy"
Under Eye – "I am beginning to feel sleepy"
Under Nose – "I am beginning to feel sleepy"
Under Lip - "I am beginning to feel sleepy"
Collar Bone - "I am beginning to feel sleepy"
Under Arm - "I am beginning to feel sleepy"
Top of Head - "I am beginning to feel sleepy"

Once you have completed this round of tapping re-evaluate yourself again and do another round of tapping appropriate to your stress level unless you have already completed three rounds of tapping.

A Tapping Script for Sleep and Insomnia Levels of 1 - 4

Begin by using the fingers of one of your hands to tap the karate chop point of the other while saying the following set up statement three times:

"I am feeling tired, my mind is calm, and I am ready for a good night's sleep"

Now use two fingers to tap each of the healing points below three to seven times saying the following reminder phrase:

"I am now ready for a good nights sleep"

A complete round of tapping for this reminder phrase would look like this:

Top of Head – "I am now ready for a good nights sleep"
Eyebrow Point – "I am now ready for a good nights sleep"
Side of Eye - "I am now ready for a good nights sleep"
Under Eye – "I am now ready for a good nights sleep"
Under Nose - "I am now ready for a good nights sleep"
Under Lip - "I am now ready for a good nights sleep"
Collar Bone - "I am now ready for a good nights sleep"
Under Arm - "I am now ready for a good nights sleep"

Top of Head - "I am now ready for a good nights sleep"

Once you have completed this round of tapping re-evaluate yourself again and do another round of tapping appropriate to your stress level unless you have already completed three rounds of tapping.

A Tapping Solution for Happiness

Most people are as happy as they make their minds to be – Abraham Lincoln

What makes people happy? Without thinking about it most people would instantly guess that it is their circumstances, but they'd be wrong. There are countless numbers of people in this world who are attractive, rich and famous and yet are actually miserable. On the other hand there are people with virtually nothing who always seem to have a smile on their face. What makes people happy?

Modern science has determined that we all have a "happiness set point" that we tend to gravitate to. This means that no matter what happens to us, good or bad, we tend to drift back to this point regardless. The aim of this energy healing script is to use our subconscious minds to raise our own individual happiness set points. It turns out that honest Abe was right, we are as happy as we intend to be.

Self-Evaluation

How happy are you right now? Rank yourself on a scale of 1 to 10, with 1 representing you are not feeling happy and a 10 representing bliss. Write down your number and let's get started.

A Tapping Script for Happiness Levels of 1 - 4

Begin by using the fingers of one of your hands to tap the karate chop point of the other while saying the following set up statement three times:

"Even though I am not happy and my life sucks I deeply and completely accept myself "

Now use two fingers to tap each of the healing points below three to seven times saying the following reminder phrase:

"There is nothing in my life to be happy about"

A complete round of tapping for this reminder phrase would look like this:

Top of Head – "There is nothing in my life to be happy about"
Eyebrow Point – "There is nothing in my life to be happy about"
Side of Eye - "There is nothing in my life to be happy about"
Under Eye – "There is nothing in my life to be happy about"
Under Nose - "There is nothing in my life to be happy about"
Under Lip - "There is nothing in my life to be happy about"
Collar Bone - "There is nothing in my life to be happy about"
Under Arm - "There is nothing in my life to be happy about"
Top of Head - "There is nothing in my life to be happy about"

Once you have completed this round of tapping re-evaluate yourself again and do another round of tapping appropriate to your stress level unless you have already completed three rounds of tapping.

A Tapping Script for Happiness Levels of 5 - 7

Begin by using the fingers of one of your hands to tap the karate chop point of the other while saying the following set up statement three times:

"I am beginning to feel better and I am open to allowing happiness into my life"

Now use two fingers to tap each of the healing points below three to seven times saying the following reminder phrase:

"I am allowing myself to feel happiness"

A complete round of tapping for this reminder phrase would look like this:

Top of Head – "I am allowing myself to feel happiness"
Eyebrow Point – "I am allowing myself to feel happiness"
Side of Eye - "I am allowing myself to feel happiness"
Under Eye – "I am allowing myself to feel happiness"
Under Nose - "I am allowing myself to feel happiness"
Under Lip - "I am allowing myself to feel happiness"
Collar Bone - "I am allowing myself to feel happiness"
Under Arm - "I am allowing myself to feel happiness"
Top of Head - "I am allowing myself to feel happiness"

Once you have completed this round of tapping re-evaluate yourself again and do another round of tapping appropriate to your stress level unless you have already completed three rounds of tapping.

A Tapping Script for Happiness Levels of 8 - 10

Begin by using the fingers of one of your hands to tap the karate chop point of the other while saying the following set up statement three times:

"I am feeling happy and I'm excited about the possibilities in my life"

Now use two fingers to tap each of the healing points below three to seven times saying the following reminder phrase:

"I am excited about life's possibilities"

A complete round of tapping for this reminder phrase would look like this:

Top of Head – "I am excited about life's possibilities"
Eyebrow Point – "I am excited about life's possibilities"
Side of Eye - "I am excited about life's possibilities"
Under Eye – "I am excited about life's possibilities"
Under Nose - "I am excited about life's possibilities"
Under Lip - "I am excited about life's possibilities"
Collar Bone - "I am excited about life's possibilities"
Under Arm - "I am excited about life's possibilities."
Top of Head - "I am excited about life's possibilities."

Once you have completed this round of tapping re-evaluate yourself again and do another round of tapping appropriate to your stress level unless you have already completed three rounds of tapping.

A Tapping Solution for Creativity

Don't think. Thinking is the enemy of creativity. It's self-conscious, and anything self-conscious is lousy. You can't try to do things. You simply must do things. – Ray Bradbury

Where do new ideas come from? In my opinion, it is the sub-conscious mind that is the wellspring from which all of your creative thoughts flow as it has access to the wisdom of the universe. The problem that most people have, and that Ray Bradbury is talking about, is that they over-think things. They allow their analytical conscious mind to overwhelm their creative sub-conscious mind. When do really great ideas come to you? Typically when you are not really thinking about it, I suspect. When you allow your sub-conscious mind some time to breathe ideas will literally manifest themselves in your brain, seemingly out of nowhere. Allowing this process to happen is what this meridian tapping script is designed to do.

Self-Evaluation

How creative are you feeling right now? If you feel like you are suffering from a serious creative block you should place yourself at the 1 to 4 range. When you are bursting with ideas you will be in the 8 to 10 range. Make a note in your notebook about how you feel and begin tapping at the appropriate level.

A Tapping Script for Happiness Levels of 1 - 4

Begin by using the fingers of one of your hands to tap the karate chop point of the other while saying the following set up statement three times:

"Even though I have a lot of trouble with creativity and I feel mentally blocked I deeply and completely accept and love myself"

Now use two fingers to tap each of the healing points below three to seven times saying the following reminder phrase:

"I am so frustrated with my creativity"

A complete round of tapping for this reminder phrase would look like this:

Top of Head – "I am so frustrated with my creativity"
Eyebrow Point – "I am so frustrated with my creativity"
Side of Eye - "I am so frustrated with my creativity"
Under Eye – "I am so frustrated with my creativity"
Under Nose - "I am so frustrated with my creativity"
Under Lip - "I am so frustrated with my creativity"
Collar Bone - "I am so frustrated with my creativity"
Under Arm - "I am so frustrated with my creativity"

Top of Head - "I am so frustrated with my creativity"

Once you have completed this round of tapping re-evaluate yourself again and do another round of tapping appropriate to your creativity level unless you have already completed three rounds of tapping.

A Tapping Script for Happiness Levels of 5 - 7

Begin by using the fingers of one of your hands to tap the karate chop point of the other while saying the following set up statement three times:

"I believe I have the power to relax which will allow my creativity to flow"

Now use two fingers to tap each of the healing points below three to seven times saying the following reminder phrase:

"I am allowing my creativity to flow"

A complete round of tapping for this reminder phrase would look like this:

Top of Head – "I am allowing my creativity to flow"
Eyebrow Point – "I am allowing my creativity to flow"
Side of Eye - "I am allowing my creativity to flow"
Under Eye – "I am allowing my creativity to flow"
Under Nose - "I am allowing my creativity to flow"
Under Lip - "I am allowing my creativity to flow"
Collar Bone - "I am allowing my creativity to flow"
Under Arm - "I am allowing my creativity to flow"
Top of Head - "I am allowing my creativity to flow"

Once you have completed this round of tapping re-evaluate yourself again and do another round of tapping appropriate to your creativity level unless you have already completed three rounds of tapping.

A Tapping Script for Happiness Levels of 8 - 10

Begin by using the fingers of one of your hands to tap the karate chop point of the other while saying the following set up statement three times:

"I have access to the knowledge of the universe, and creative ideas and thoughts flow effortlessly through me"

Now use two fingers to tap each of the healing points below three to seven times saying the following reminder phrase:

"Creative ideas and thoughts flow through me"

A complete round of tapping for this reminder phrase would look like this:

Top of Head – "Creative ideas and thoughts flow through me"
Eyebrow Point – "Creative ideas and thoughts flow through me"
Side of Eye - "Creative ideas and thoughts flow through me"
Under Eye – "Creative ideas and thoughts flow through me"
Under Nose -"Creative ideas and thoughts flow through me"
Under Lip - "Creative ideas and thoughts flow through me"
Collar Bone - "Creative ideas and thoughts flow through me"
Under Arm - "Creative ideas and thoughts flow through me"

Top of Head - "Creative ideas and thoughts flow through me"

Once you have completed this round of tapping re-evaluate yourself again and do another round of tapping appropriate to your creativity level unless you have already completed three rounds of tapping.

A Tapping Solution for Shyness

I think we all have blocks between us and the best version of ourselves whether it's shyness, insecurity, anxiety, whether it's a physical block, and the story of a person overcoming that block to their best self. It's truly inspiring because I think all of us are engaged in that every day. – Tom Hooper

If you feel shy or uncomfortable in social situations you are not alone. Many famous people such as Steve Martin and Marilyn Manson have admitted they became performers to overcome their shyness. In and of itself there is nothing wrong with being a little shy, but too much shyness can prevent you from seizing opportunities in both your personal and professional life. This meridian tapping technique will help you cross this bridge.

Self-Evaluation

Imagine that you are in a social situation surrounded by strangers...now how do you feel? If the thought of interacting with anyone terrifies you, rank yourself as an 8 to 10. A ranking of 1 to 4 indicates a comfort and openness to interacting with others, which is what we are striving for.

A Tapping Script for Shyness Levels of 8 - 10

Begin by using the fingers of one of your hands to tap the karate chop point of the other while saying the following set up statement three times:

"Even though I am shy and uncomfortable around people I deeply and completely love and accept myself"

Now use two fingers to tap each of the healing points below three to seven times saying the following reminder phrase:

"I am shy and uncomfortable around people"

A complete round of tapping for this reminder phrase would look like this:

Top of Head – "I am shy and uncomfortable around people"
Eyebrow Point – "I am shy and uncomfortable around people"
Side of Eye - "I am shy and uncomfortable around people"
Under Eye – "I am shy and uncomfortable around people"
Under Nose - "I am shy and uncomfortable around people"
Under Lip - "I am shy and uncomfortable around people"
Collar Bone - "I am shy and uncomfortable around people"
Under Arm - "I am shy and uncomfortable around people"

Top of Head - "I am shy and uncomfortable around people"

Once you have completed this round of tapping re-evaluate yourself again and do another round of tapping appropriate to your shyness level unless you have already completed three rounds of tapping.

A Tapping Script for Shyness Levels of 5 - 7

Begin by using the fingers of one of your hands to tap the karate chop point of the other while saying the following set up statement three times:

"Even though I am shy and uncomfortable in social situations I believe I can handle it"

Now use two fingers to tap each of the healing points below three to seven times saying the following reminder phrase:

"I am learning to be comfortable around people"

A complete round of tapping for this reminder phrase would look like this:

Top of Head – "I am learning to be comfortable around people"
Eyebrow Point – "I am learning to be comfortable around people"
Side of Eye - "I am learning to be comfortable around people"
Under Eye – "I am learning to be comfortable around people"
Under Nose - "I am learning to be comfortable around people"
Under Lip - "I am learning to be comfortable around people"
Collar Bone - "I am learning to be comfortable around people"
Under Arm - "I am learning to be comfortable around people"

Top of Head - "I am learning to be comfortable around people"

Once you have completed this round of tapping re-evaluate yourself again and do another round of tapping appropriate to your shyness level unless you have already completed three rounds of tapping.

A Tapping Script for Shyness Levels of 1 - 4

Begin by using the fingers of one of your hands to tap the karate chop point of the other while saying the following set up statement three times:

"I am a strong and confident person and I am comfortable in social situations"

Now use two fingers to tap each of the healing points below three to seven times saying the following reminder phrase:

"I am comfortable in social situations"

A complete round of tapping for this reminder phrase would look like this:

Top of Head – "I am comfortable in social situations"
Eyebrow Point – "I am comfortable in social situations"
Side of Eye - "I am comfortable in social situations"
Under Eye – "I am comfortable in social situations"
Under Nose - "I am comfortable in social situations"
Under Lip - "I am comfortable in social situations"
Collar Bone - "I am comfortable in social situations"
Under Arm - "I am comfortable in social situations"
Top of Head - "I am comfortable in social situations"

Once you have completed this round of tapping re-evaluate yourself again and do another round of tapping appropriate to your shyness level, unless you have already completed three rounds of tapping.

A Tapping Solution for Procrastination

Procrastination is one of the most common and deadliest diseases and its toll on success and happiness is heavy – Wayne Gretzky

We all have things we know we should do, things that we know will help us in the long term if we get them done. Why do we put them off? All of us are prone to some procrastination at some point, but extreme procrastination can severely limit ourselves in our personal and professional lives. In my view, the root of procrastination is simply the brain misjudging what it perceives as short-term pain over long-term gain. This tapping script is designed to fix this mental short circuit.

Self-Evaluation

How much of a procrastinator are you? If you are extremely prone to putting things off give yourself a rating of 8 to 10. Our goal is to get you down to a 1 or 2, which would mean you rarely procrastinate at all and simply get things done.

A Tapping Script for Procrastinating Levels of 8 - 10

Begin by using the fingers of one of your hands to tap the karate chop point of the other while saying the following set up statement three times:

"Even though I have been procrastinating I deeply and completely love and accept myself"

Now use two fingers to tap each of the healing points below three to seven times saying the following reminder phrase:

"I don't know why, but I keep procrastinating"

A complete round of tapping for this reminder phrase would look like this:

Top of Head – "I don't know why, but I keep procrastinating"
Eyebrow Point – "I don't know why, but I keep procrastinating"
Side of Eye - "I don't know why, but I keep procrastinating"
Under Eye – "I don't know why, but I keep procrastinating"
Under Nose - "I don't know why, but I keep procrastinating"
Under Lip - "I don't know why, but I keep procrastinating"
Collar Bone - "I don't know why, but I keep procrastinating"
Under Arm - "I don't know why, but I keep procrastinating"

Top of Head - "I don't know why, but I keep procrastinating"

Once you have completed this round of tapping re-evaluate yourself again and do another round of tapping appropriate to for your procrastination level, unless you have already completed three rounds of tapping.

A Tapping Script for Procrastinating Levels of 5 - 7

Begin by using the fingers of one of your hands to tap the karate chop point of the other while saying the following set up statement three times:

"I understand that my habit of procrastination is under my control and I am overcoming it"

Now use two fingers to tap each of the healing points below three to seven times saying the following reminder phrase:

"My procrastination is under my control"

A complete round of tapping for this reminder phrase would look like this:

Top of Head – "My procrastination is under my control"
Eyebrow Point – "My procrastination is under my control"
Side of Eye - "My procrastination is under my control"
Under Eye – "My procrastination is under my control"
Under Nose - "My procrastination is under my control"
Under Lip - "My procrastination is under my control"
Collar Bone - "My procrastination is under my control"
Under Arm - "My procrastination is under my control"

Top of Head - "My procrastination is under my control"

Once you have completed this round of tapping re-evaluate yourself again and do another round of tapping appropriate to for your procrastination level, unless you have already completed three rounds of tapping.

A Tapping Script for Procrastination Levels of 1 - 4

Begin by using the fingers of one of your hands to tap the karate chop point of the other while saying the following set up statement three times:

"I no longer allow myself to procrastinate and I get things done right away"

Now use two fingers to tap each of the healing points below three to seven times saying the following reminder phrase:

"I get things done right away"

A complete round of tapping for this reminder phrase would look like this:

Top of Head – "I get things done right away"
Eyebrow Point – "I get things done right away"
Side of Eye - "I get things done right away"
Under Eye – "I get things done right away"
Under Nose - "I get things done right away"
Under Lip - "I get things done right away"
Collar Bone - "I get things done right away"
Under Arm - "I get things done right away"
Top of Head - "I get things done right away"

Once you have completed this round of tapping re-evaluate yourself again and do another round of tapping appropriate to for your procrastination level, unless you have already completed three rounds of tapping.

A Tapping Solution for Confidence

Optimism is the faith that leads to achievement. Nothing can be done without hope and confidence. – Helen Keller

When put into unfamiliar circumstances even the bravest of us can feel a little unsure of ourselves. The quality that gets you through those moments is confidence, confidence in your abilities, confidence in your strength, and confidence in yourself. The goal of this meridian tapping script is to install this quality in you so that you can handle whatever life throws at you, come what may.

Self-Evaluation

Take a deep breath and imagine a time when you were in a challenging situation. How confident did you feel? If you didn't feel very confident give yourself a 1 to a 4. A ranking of 10 indicates superhuman confidence in your abilities, which is the goal we are striving for.

A Tapping Script for Confidence Levels 1 - 4

Begin by using the fingers of one of your hands to tap the karate chop point of the other while saying the following set up statement three times:

"Even though in the past I haven't been very confident, I choose to love and accept myself"

Now use two fingers to tap each of the healing points below three to seven times saying the following reminder phrase:

"I am not very confident"

A complete round of tapping for this reminder phrase would look like this:

Top of Head – "I am not very confident"
Eyebrow Point – "I am not very confident"
Side of Eye - "I am not very confident"
Under Eye – "I am not very confident"
Under Nose - "I am not very confident"
Under Lip - "I am not very confident"
Collar Bone - "I am not very confident"
Under Arm - "I am not very confident"
Top of Head - "I am not very confident"

Once you have completed this round of tapping re-evaluate yourself again and do another round of tapping appropriate for your self-perceived confidence level, unless you have already completed three rounds of tapping.

A Tapping Script for Confidence Levels 5 - 7

Begin by using the fingers of one of your hands to tap the karate chop point of the other while saying the following set up statement three times:

"I am allowing myself to feel confident and I believe I can handle anything"

Now use two fingers to tap each of the healing points below three to seven times saying the following reminder phrase:

"I am allowing myself to feel confident"

A complete round of tapping for this reminder phrase would look like this:

Top of Head – "I am allowing myself to feel confident"
Eyebrow Point – "I am allowing myself to feel confident"
Side of Eye - "I am allowing myself to feel confident"
Under Eye – "I am allowing myself to feel confident"
Under Nose - "I am allowing myself to feel confident"
Under Lip - "I am allowing myself to feel confident"
Collar Bone - "I am allowing myself to feel confident"
Under Arm - "I am allowing myself to feel confident"
Top of Head - "I am allowing myself to feel confident"

Once you have completed this round of tapping re-evaluate yourself again and do another round of tapping appropriate for your self-perceived confidence level, unless you have already completed three rounds of tapping.

A Tapping Script for Confidence Levels 8 - 10

Begin by using the fingers of one of your hands to tap the karate chop point of the other while saying the following set up statement three times:

"I possess a quiet confidence as I know I can handle anything life throws at me"

Now use two fingers to tap each of the healing points below three to seven times saying the following reminder phrase:

"I know I can handle anything"

A complete round of tapping for this reminder phrase would look like this:

Top of Head – "I know I can handle anything"
Eyebrow Point – "I know I can handle anything"
Side of Eye - "I know I can handle anything"
Under Eye – "I know I can handle anything"
Under Nose - "I know I can handle anything"
Under Lip - "I know I can handle anything"
Collar Bone - "I know I can handle anything"
Under Arm - "I know I can handle anything"
Top of Head - "I know I can handle anything"

Once you have completed this round of tapping re-evaluate yourself again and do another round of tapping appropriate for your self-perceived confidence level, unless you have already completed three rounds of tapping.

A Tapping Solution for Making Life Easier

The path before you is clear, why do you throw stones? – Buddha

If asked, most of us would say that they like it when things go smoothly, when things are easier. This is what our conscious minds say, at least. If this is true then why do so many of us complicate even the simplest tasks? Once again it comes down to the part of our brain that is really in charge, our subconscious mind. Without you even being aware of it your brains engineer has been picking up messages like "No pain, no gain!" and "Nothing good in life comes easy!" This conflict is why we so often sabotage ourselves in any number of ways even when the road before us is clear. It's why people throw stones ahead of themselves when they are walking their paths. This round of meridian tapping is designed to reprogram your subconscious mind so that it doesn't see everything as being hard. When this happens and your conscious and subconscious minds are able to truly work together your life will simply start to flow. It will literally just become easier.

Self-Evaluation

Take a few deep breaths and mediate on how hard you think life is or has been for you. If you see life as being a constant struggle you are in the 1 – 4 zone. Feeling like your life is flowing naturally and easily is the opposite end of the scale and is what we want to get to. Let's get started walking that path.

A Tapping Script for Making Life Easier Levels 1 - 4

Begin by using the fingers of one of your hands to tap the karate chop point of the other while saying the following set up statement three times:

"Even though I hold the belief that life has to be a constant struggle, I choose to love and accept myself completely"

Now use two fingers to tap each of the healing points below three to seven times saying the following reminder phrase:

"I deserve to have a hard life"

A complete round of tapping for this reminder phrase would look like this:

Top of Head – "I deserve to have a hard life"
Eyebrow Point – "I deserve to have a hard life"
Side of Eye - "I deserve to have a hard life"
Under Eye – "I deserve to have a hard life"
Under Nose - "I deserve to have a hard life"
Under Lip - "I deserve to have a hard life"
Collar Bone - "I deserve to have a hard life"
Under Arm - "I deserve to have a hard life"
Top of Head - "I deserve to have a hard life"

Once you have completed this round of tapping re-evaluate yourself again and do another round of tapping appropriate for your self-perceived "Easy life" level, unless you have already completed three rounds of tapping.

A Tapping Script for Making Life Easier Levels 5 - 7

Begin by using the fingers of one of your hands to tap the karate chop point of the other while saying the following set up statement three times:

"Even though in the past I have believed that life had to be a struggle I am beginning to realize it doesn't. I am worthy of more"

Now use two fingers to tap each of the healing points below three to seven times saying the following reminder phrase:

"I want to make things easier"

A complete round of tapping for this reminder phrase would look like this:

Top of Head – "I want to make things easier"
Eyebrow Point – "I want to make things easier"
Side of Eye - "I want to make things easier"
Under Eye – "I want to make things easier"
Under Nose - "I want to make things easier"
Under Lip - "I want to make things easier"
Collar Bone - "I want to make things easier"
Under Arm - "I want to make things easier"
Top of Head - "I want to make things easier"

Once you have completed this round of tapping re-evaluate yourself again and do another round of tapping appropriate for your self-perceived "Easy life" level, unless you have already completed three rounds of tapping.

A Tapping Script for Making Life Easier Levels 8 - 10

Begin by using the fingers of one of your hands to tap the karate chop point of the other while saying the following set up statement three times:

"My life is becoming easier and I am excited by the possibilities that are constantly opening up for me"

Now use two fingers to tap each of the healing points below three to seven times saying the following reminder phrase:

"I am excited about life's possibilities"

A complete round of tapping for this reminder phrase would look like this:

Top of Head – "I am excited about life's possibilities"
Eyebrow Point – "I am excited about life's possibilities"
Side of Eye - "I am excited about life's possibilities"
Under Eye – "I am excited about life's possibilities"
Under Nose - "I am excited about life's possibilities"
Under Lip - "I am excited about life's possibilities"
Collar Bone - "I am excited about life's possibilities"
Under Arm - "I am excited about life's possibilities"

Top of Head - "I am excited about life's possibilities"

Once you have completed this round of tapping re-evaluate yourself again and do another round of tapping appropriate for your self-perceived "Easy life" level unless you have already completed three rounds of tapping.

A Tapping Solution for Love

*Keep love in your heart. A life without it is like a sunless garden when the flowers are dead –
Oscar Wilde*

What is life without love? It is something everything human heart desires, yet too many of us are utterly closed of to it. The roots of this condition are often in childhood. Ideally their parents provide a person's first experience with real love, but this isn't always the case. Parents are people and they can be overworked and overwhelmed by life just as easily as the rest of us. This can result in a less than affectionate childhood. However, even in cases where the parents were kind and loving there are a myriad of negative experiences one can have later in life that can close your mind to love's possibilities.

For whatever reason, we have closed this mental state, which prevents us from seeing the love that exists all around us. Walking down the street you are likely to see lonely and discouraged people while the couple holding hands or the friends enjoying each other's company will be all but invisible to you. This is what we want to change.

Self-Evaluation

Take a few deep breaths and mediate on how open to love you feel.
If you feel that you life is relatively empty of love you are in the 1 – 4 zone. Feeling that love is all around you is the opposite end of the

scale and is what we want to get to. Let's get started walking that path.

A Tapping Script for Love Levels 1 - 4

Begin by using the fingers of one of your hands to tap the karate chop point of the other while saying the following set up statement three times:

"Even though I feel shut down to love, and I don't notice it around me, I'm open to seeing and experiencing it more in my life"

Now use two fingers to tap each of the healing points below three to seven times saying the following reminder phrase:

"I don't want to experience love"

A complete round of tapping for this reminder phrase would look like this:

Top of Head – "I don't want to experience love"
Eyebrow Point – "I don't want to experience love"
Side of Eye - "I don't want to experience love"
Under Eye – "I don't want to experience love"
Under Nose - "I don't want to experience love"
Under Lip - ""I don't want to experience love"
Collar Bone - "I don't want to experience love"
Under Arm - "I don't want to experience love"
Top of Head - "I don't want to experience love"

Once you have completed this round of tapping re-evaluate yourself again and do another round of tapping appropriate for your self-perceived "Love" level, unless you have already completed three rounds of tapping.

A Tapping Script for Love Levels 5 - 7

Begin by using the fingers of one of your hands to tap the karate chop point of the other while saying the following set up statement three times:

"I am open to love and I am allowing more love into my life everyday."

Now use two fingers to tap each of the healing points below three to seven times saying the following reminder phrase:

"I am open to seeing and experiencing love"

A complete round of tapping for this reminder phrase would look like this:

Top of Head – "I am open to seeing and experiencing love"
Eyebrow Point – "I am open to seeing and experiencing love"
Side of Eye - "I am open to seeing and experiencing love"
Under Eye – "I am open to seeing and experiencing love"
Under Nose - "I am open to seeing and experiencing love"
Under Lip - "I am open to seeing and experiencing love"
Collar Bone - "I am open to seeing and experiencing love"
Under Arm - "I am open to seeing and experiencing love"
Top of Head - "I am open to seeing and experiencing love"

Once you have completed this round of tapping re-evaluate yourself again and do another round of tapping appropriate for your self-perceived "Love" level, unless you have already completed three rounds of tapping.

A Tapping Script for Love Levels 8 - 10

Begin by using the fingers of one of your hands to tap the karate chop point of the other while saying the following set up statement three times:

"I am a loving person and I effortlessly radiate and receive love."

Now use two fingers to tap each of the healing points below three to seven times saying the following reminder phrase:

"I enjoy radiating and receiving love."

A complete round of tapping for this reminder phrase would look like this:

Top of Head – "I enjoy radiating and receiving love."
Eyebrow Point – "I enjoy radiating and receiving love.""
Side of Eye - "I enjoy radiating and receiving love."
Under Eye – "I enjoy radiating and receiving love."
Under Nose - "I enjoy radiating and receiving love."
Under Lip - "I enjoy radiating and receiving love."
Collar Bone - "I enjoy radiating and receiving love."
Under Arm - "I enjoy radiating and receiving love."
Top of Head "I enjoy radiating and receiving love."

Once you have completed this round of tapping re-evaluate yourself again and do another round of tapping appropriate for your self-perceived "Love" level, unless you have already completed three rounds of tapping.

Your Journey is Just Beginning

The most successful people recognize that in life they create their own love, they manufacture their own meaning, they generate their own motivation
– Neil Degrasse Tyson

Although you are now almost at the end of this book you are really only at the starting line for what tapping can do for you. It is my fondest hope that you now possess the knowledge of how your mind processes information and how tapping can allow you to re-program your cause and effect computer when needed. The sample tapping scripts that you have read are a great starting point, but that's all they really are. They are like the training wheels on a bike. They are designed to give you confidence but when you know what you are doing they are ultimately unnecessary. I'm sure that after you read through them all you probably thought to yourself, "Is this all there is to it? I can do this!" and indeed you can. Your next steps are ones you will have to take by yourself in order to make tapping your own. What are your own unique challenges and goals? Whatever they are I hope you feel confident now to make your own tapping scripts and tackle them head on. I have faith that you now have the tools to burst through whatever invisible barriers have been holding you back. It's time to take the training wheels off and ride on your own. Your new life is waiting for you.

My hand in yours,
Anthony Anholt

FAQ

How often should I tap?

This is probably the most common question associated with meridian tapping and there really is no one right answer. If you were just starting out, I would recommend doing a minimum of 3 rounds of tapping once a day. My personal preference is first thing in the morning or right before you go to sleep. Do this for a couple of weeks at least. From there, judge how you are feeling. Some people find that doing a few rounds of tapping 2 or 3 times a day works best for them. It's really up to you. Just remember that tapping is so simple you can really do it almost anywhere. As well you don't need to limit yourself to doing the 3 tapping rounds as outlined in the "A Tapping Solution For ..." scripts. If you are feeling good and you have the time feel free to do more. Ultimately it really is up to you and how you feel.

One of the most common phrases that I have read in yours and others EFT scripts are "I love and accept myself". I wish I did, but I simply don't. What can I do?

First of all do not let the fact that you can't say this phrase to yourself honestly upset you. You are not alone in experiencing this. Just know that other people have started out where you are and have gotten through it too. It just takes time.

Here are some options for you to try:

1. You can just say it anyway. Even if it feels untrue to you now if you just keep saying it your subconscious mind will eventually start to believe it.
2. You can make the phrase your own by softening it. For example, you could say, "I am learning to deeply and completely love and accept myself" or "I am in the process of learning how to deeply and completely love and accept myself".
3. You could create a tapping script based just on this. Set Up Phrase – "Even though I can't say I deeply and completely love and accept myself I am open to finding a way to care and accept who I am now". Reminder Phrase – "I am working on loving myself".

I'm not sure I'm buying any of this. Isn't this just the Placebo Effect in action?

Let's say you're right. If so, so what? Even if you are getting results just because of the Placebo Effect, don't you care more about the results? Just because the cause might be related to the Placebo Effect doesn't mean that the effect itself isn't real. Having said that though so many therapists are now using EFT techniques it seems highly unlikely that energy tapping is just merely a "Placebo Effect". Research psychologists at various universities are conducting double blind experiments on this technique as you read this, but these take time. You can wait if you want, but if EFT tapping is working for you now, why stop?

I've been tapping for a while now and my condition is so much better I really don't think I need the medicine my doctor prescribed me. Is it OK if I go off them?

Absolutely not! Congratulations on your progress but if you are taking any kind of prescription medicine NEVER change the dosage without first consulting with your doctor, period.

Do I need to see a therapist to use tapping and energy healing?

Tapping is like a lot of things. It is not a complicated technique and most people do just fine by themselves. However it never hurts to have a coach when you are learning something new. If you feel you are not making the progress you like seeing a therapist who specializes in energy tapping can be an asset.

Should I tap with one hand or two?

When you are tapping sometimes there are two healing points you can tap on, such as on the side of the eye. Again it comes down to personal preference. After experimenting I like to use both hands to tap both points when available. However if you prefer to use one hand there is nothing wrong with that. Do what works for you.

Which karate chop point should I tap on, my right or left?

Again it doesn't really matter, but what I like to do is to tap on my right hand for the first round of tapping, then tap on my left for the second round. I like to do it this way as I feel it gives my tapping a sense of symmetry.

Why do I stop tapping when it appears to be working for me?

This is not uncommon and is an issue that many dieters face. You are making progress towards your goal but as you approach it a feeling of (often deserved) satisfaction sweeps over you. The issue you were confronting doesn't appear to be nearly as daunting, you're feeling better, and so you start to slack off. This is a very human reaction and it's something we're all guilty of from time to time. The only thing I can suggest is to always keep your eye on the prize. Also creating your own unique tapping script involving your desire to complete what you started wouldn't be a bad idea either.

For the various scripts found in this book sometimes you start at the lower end of the scale (1 – 4) and other times at the high end (8 – 10). This lack of consistency bugs me.

I've tailored the scales for the various scripts to what I think works best for the individual issues being addressed. For example I think if you are experiencing low love levels a ranking of 1 – 4 makes more sense. However if you are a world-class procrastinator starting at 8 – 10 makes more sense to me as this is a quality you want to reduce. You can always change my scale system if you wish, but it feels right to me.

One of your tapping scripts says A when I think B makes more sense.

Great! If you find a phrase that speaks to you more than what I've written by all means use it. I've said it before and I'll say it gain, your ultimate goal should be to make tapping your own. The energy healing scripts you have read in this book, or anywhere else for that matter, did not come down from some mountain written on stone tablets. They are meant as a starting point and a guide only. Once you get more comfortable with your own tapping abilities by all means experiment and change things up. That is the ultimate goal.

I really thought it was interesting how you described how the conscious and subconscious minds work. If I wanted to read more about this what book would you recommend?

In my mind there is one acknowledged master in this area on whose shoulders everyone else stands. That man is Maxwell Maltz. His book is entitled [Psycho-Cybernetics](#) and it is well worth reading.

Other Books Of Interest

Health is a large word. It embraces not the body only, but the mind and spirit as well...and not today's pain or pleasure alone, but the whole being and outlook of a man. - James H. West

If you are interested in reading more about the subject of energy tapping or related health issues you will likely find these books worthwhile.

The Tapping Solution: A Revolutionary System for Stress-Free Living by Nick Ortner

The EFT Manual, 2nd Ed. By Gary Craig

The Tapping Cure: A Revolutionary System for Rapid Relief from Phobias, Anxiety, Post-Traumatic Stress Disorder and More by Roberta Temes Ph.D.

The 10 Best-Ever Anxiety Management Techniques: Understanding How Your Brain Makes You Anxious and What You Can Do to Change It by Margaret Wehrenberg

I've heard from many people with anxiety issues that this book is particularly helpful.

The Relaxation and Stress Reduction Workbook by Mathew McKay, Martha Davis, Elizabeth Eshelman and Patrick Fanning

Energy Medicine: Balancing Your Body's Energies for Optimal Health, Joy, and

Vitality Updated and Expanded by Donna Eden, David Feinstein and Caroline Myss

Freedom at Your Fingertips: Get Rapid Physical and Emotional Relief with the Breakthrough System of Tapping by Ron Ball and Joseph Mercola

Emotional Freedom: Liberate Yourself from Negative Emotions and Transform Your Life by Judith Orloff

For whatever reason Judith Orloff doesn't seem to be getting as much attention as Nick Ortner but this is nonetheless an excellent book

Discover The Power Of Meridian Tapping; A Revolutionary Method For Stress-Free Living by Patricia Carrington

About The Author

Anthony Anholt has been interested and involved in athletics and fitness for his entire life. His specialty is "gym less" workouts, or exercise systems that do not require any kind of special equipment. He is also interested in enhancing performance in all sports and natural healing techniques. This is his sixth book.

One Last Thing

You've now reached the end of the book and I sincerely hope it will provide you with the means to achieve your dreams. If you did find it useful I would very much appreciate it if you could take 5 minutes and write a short review for it on Amazon or wherever you purchased it. Even a couple of sentences would be immensely helpful to me. Regardless I want to thank-you once again for purchasing my book and I wish you all the best in the future.

CPSIA information can be obtained at www.ICGtesting.com
Printed in the USA
LVOW04s2155110215

426641LV00029B/1580/P